D1528964

DR. BOB'S
AMAZING WORLD OF
ANIMALS
RHINOCEROSES

By Ruth Owen

WINDMILL
BOOKS
New York

Published in 2012 by Windmill Books, An Imprint of Rosen Publishing
29 East 21st Street, New York, NY 10010

Editor for Ruby Tuesday Books Ltd: Mark J. Sachner
U.S. Editor: Sara Antill
Designer: Trudi Webb

Photo Credits: Cover, 1, 4–5, 6–7, 10–11, 12–13, 14–15, 16–17, 18–19, 20–21, 22–23, 24–25, 26–27, 30 © Shutterstock; 8, 9 (top) © Wikipedia Creative Commons (public domain); 9 (bottom) © Press Association Images; 29 © FLPA.

Library of Congress Cataloging-in-Publication Data

Owen, Ruth, 1967–
 Rhinoceroses / by Ruth Owen.
     p. cm. — (Dr. Bob's amazing world of animals)
 Includes index.
 ISBN 978-1-61533-550-3 (library binding) — ISBN 978-1-61533-560-2 (pbk.) —
ISBN 978-1-61533-561-9 (6-pack)
 1. Rhinoceroses—Juvenile literature. I. Title.
 QL737.U63O94 2012
 599.66'8—dc23
                                        2011030373

Manufactured in the United States of America

CPSIA Compliance Information: Batch #RTW2102WM: For Further Information contact Windmill Books, New York, New York at 1-866-478-0556

Contents

The Rhinoceros

Welcome to my amazing world of animals. Today, we will be finding out about an animal that has been on Earth for about 50 million years — the rhinoceros!

Black rhinos

Let's investigate...

Hank's
WOOF OF WISDOM!

There are five types of rhino:
- White rhino
- Black rhino
- Greater one-horned rhino
- Sumatran rhino
- Javan rhino

Both white and black rhinos are actually gray!

White rhinos may
have gotten their
name by accident.

White rhinos

Wide lip

British visitors to Africa heard local people calling the
rhinos "weidt." They thought the word meant "white."
It actually means "wide." The local people were
describing the rhino's wide upper lip!

The African Rhino Files

White and black rhinos live in Africa.
Both types of rhino are in danger.

White Rhino

- Lives on **grasslands**.

- Height to shoulder: up to 6 feet (1.8 m)

- Weight (female): up to 2.2 tons (2 t)

- Weight (male): up to 2.8 tons (2.5 t)

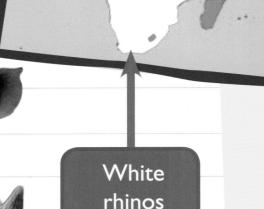

Africa

Atlantic
Ocean

Indian
Ocean

White
rhinos
live in the
white areas.

Black Rhino

- Lives where there are trees and bushes to eat. It can be found on grasslands, in deserts, and in forests.

- Height to shoulder: up to 5.3 feet (1.6 m)

- Weight (female): up to 1 ton (1 t)

- Weight (male): up to 1.5 tons (1.4 t)

Africa

Atlantic Ocean

Indian Ocean

Black rhinos live in the black areas.

7

The Asian Rhino Files

Three types of rhino live in Asia. They are all in danger of becoming **extinct**.

Greater one-horned rhino

- Lives in protected parks in India and Nepal.

- Height to shoulder: up to 6.5 feet (2 m)

- Weight: up to 2 tons (1.8 t)

- These rhinos are good at swimming and diving. They sometimes feed on underwater plants.

Skin folds that look like armor

Sumatran rhino

Hairy skin

- Lives in protected parks in **tropical** forests in Sumatra, Indonesia, and in Sabah, Malaysia.

- Height to shoulder: up to 4.8 feet (1.5 m)

- Weight: up to 1,763 pounds (800 kg)

- This rhino is the closest living relative to the woolly rhinoceros that lived until about 10,000 years ago.

Javan rhino

- There are fewer than 50 Javan rhinos left. They live in just two protected areas in Java, Indonesia and in Vietnam.

- Height to shoulder: up to 5.6 feet (1.7 m)

- Weight: up to 2.5 tons (2.3 t)

Rhino Horns

All rhinos have horns. Males use them to fight with other males over females.

The horns are made of thousands of hair-like strands of keratin pressed together. Keratin is the material that your fingernails are made of.

Hank's
WOOF OF WISDOM!

A white rhino's front horn may grow to be 3 feet (1 m) long!

Mother rhinos use their horns to protect their young from enemies such as lions and crocodiles.

Lip-Smacking Rhino Snacks

All rinos are **herbivores**.
This means they only eat plants.

White rhinos mostly eat grass. Their wide, square-looking upper lip munches through grass like a lawnmower!

Black rhinos eat trees and bushes. Black rhinos have a pointed upper lip.

A black rhino can move its upper lip and use it like fingers! The rhino grabs leaves and branches with its lip and pulls them into its mouth.

Pointed lip

Rhino Senses and Surprises

Rhinos cannot see very well. They can hear and smell well, though.

A rhino's ears can turn in different directions to pick up sounds.

A rhino can smell a person or another animal from about 1,300 feet (400 m) away.

**Charging
black
rhino**

Black rhinos have a reputation for charging people. This is probably because the rhinos and people meet up by accident in thick trees and bushes. The rhino charges because it is surprised!

A black rhino can run at 34 miles per hour (55 km/h)!

Rhino Skin Care

A rhino's skin looks like tough leather, but it can be harmed by the hot sun and insect bites.

Rhino skin

Hank's
WOOF OF WISDOM!

A rhino's skin may be 2 inches (5 cm) thick in places.

Rhinos spend time wallowing, or lying, in mud. A layer of mud stops insects from getting to a rhino's skin. The mud also works like sunscreen.

Oxpecker bird

Oxpecker birds sit on rhinos and eat any bugs that land on the rhinos' skin!

Rhino Babies

A female white rhino has her first baby, or calf, when she is around 6 to 7 years old. She is pregnant for 16 months.

A newborn white rhino calf can stand up in less than an hour.

A white rhino calf weighs up to 132 pounds (60 kg) when it is born!

The mother rhino feeds her calf with milk from her body.

Calf drinking milk

Rhino calves start to eat grass and plants when they are about 2 months old.

Growing Up

A rhino calf will stay with its mother for 3 or 4 years.

When it is time for the mother rhino to give birth to a new calf, she chases her older calf away.

It's tough for a young rhino when it first leaves its mother. The rhino may be attacked by a group of lions. It may try to hang out with an adult male rhino and be attacked.

Young white rhino

A black rhino mother will sometimes allow an older calf to come back when her new calf is a few months old.

21

Rhino Life

Adult male rhinos, or bulls, live alone and have their own **territory**.

Bull rhino

A male rhino **mates** with the females in his territory.

An adult male may allow teenage males to visit or live in his territory. If another adult male comes into his territory, however, there will be a fight!

Female white rhinos mostly live in pairs with their latest calf.

Female rhino (center) with her last two calves

Female black rhinos may live with their last two or three calves.

Keep Out!

Rhinos don't have fences or signs to tell other rhinos where their territories begin and end.

Black and white male rhinos kick and scrape their dung along the edges of their territories. This tells other males to keep out!

Rhino dung

Male rhinos also spray the edges of their territories with their urine.

Hank's
WOOF OF WISDOM!

Rhinos create huge piles of dung, called middens. Male and female rhinos can add to the dung piles. This is a way of sending messages to each other.

Rhinos in Danger!

About 200 years ago, there were 1 million rhinos on Earth. Today, there are fewer than 30,000.

Rhinos are killed for their horns.

Hank's
WOOF OF WISDOM!

The numbers of rhinos left are:
- White rhinos: 17,000 to 18,000
- Black rhinos: 4,000 to 5,000
- Greater one-horned rhinos: fewer than 3,000
- Sumatran rhinos: around 200
- Javan rhinos: fewer than 50

Rhino horn is used in **traditional** Chinese medicine. People believe it can cure many illnesses, but this is probably not true.

In the country of Yemen, it is traditional to own expensive daggers called *janbiyas*. Their handles are made from rhino horn.

Rhino Rangers

It is against the law to kill rhinos, but people still do it! These people are known as poachers.

Rhino rangers patrol the forests and grasslands looking for poachers.

Rangers get to know all the rhinos in an area. If a rhino is missing, they know poachers may have been in the area.

Rangers

Greater one-horned rhino

Hank's
WOOF OF WISDOM!

Poachers are less likely to attack rhinos that are being protected by rangers.

This young rhino's mother was killed. He was raised by people and now lives back in the wild.

Ranger

Glossary

extinct (ik-STINGKT)
No longer existing.

grasslands (GRAS-landz)
A hot habitat with lots of grass and few trees or bushes. Sometimes it is very dry, and at other times there is lots of rain.

herbivore (ER-buh-vor)
An animal that eats only plants.

mate (MAYT)
When a male and a female animal get together to produce young; or the word for an animal's partner.

territory (TER-uh-tor-ee)
An area that an animal protects because it is where it lives and finds food and mates.

traditional (truh-DIH-shuh-nul)
Something that a group of people have done for many years and have passed on to the people who came after them.

tropical (TRAH-puh-kul)
Having to do with the warmer parts of Earth that are near the equator.

Dr. Bob's Fast Fact Board

The word "rhinoceros" comes from the Greek words "rhino" and "ceros." The word "rhino" means "nose," and "ceros" means "horn."

A white rhino can live for up to 50 years.

The white rhino is the second-largest land animal on Earth. Only the elephant is larger.

The longest white rhino horn ever recorded measured 62 inches (1.6 m) long.

Greater one-horned rhinos have long, pointed lower teeth. Males use them in fights, and they can grow to be 3 inches (8 cm) long.

Web Sites

For Web resources related to the subject of this book, go to: **www.windmillbooks.com/weblinks** and select this book's title.

Read More

Hamilton, Garry. *Rhino Rescue: Changing the Future for Endangered Wildlife*. Ontario, Canada: Firefly Books, 2006.

Kalman, Bobbie. *Endangered Rhinoceroses*. Earth's Endangered Animals. New York: Crabtree Publishing Company, 2005.

Walden, Katherine. *Rhinoceroses*. Safari Animals. New York: PowerKids Press, 2009.

Index